ALB ERT WAT SON

I have a belief that you have a certain electrical pattern in your brain that responds to certain triggers, and that photography in my case was a trigger. It fitted me perfectly.

A. Watson

Den Fotografien von Albert Watson kann man sich kaum entziehen. Ihre Brillanz und Eindringlichkeit, ja Erhabenheit, hebt sie von der heute so exaltierten Bildwelt deutlich ab und stellt den Fotografen in die Reihe der modernen Klassiker.

Watson, der über ein Grafik- und Filmstudium zur Fotografie gekommen ist, hat in seinen Arbeiten stets verschiedene fotografische Auffassungen reflektiert, diese jedoch nie übernommen. Die Bildsprache des Fotografen folgt eigenen, unverwechselbaren Regeln und Auffassungen von Qualität. Albert Watson ist ein workoholic. In seinem Archiv in der New Yorker Washington Street versammeln sich Millionen von Bildern und Negativen. Auf den Archivalien stehen die Namen weltweit bekannter Magazine und Unternehmen. Watsons Aufnahmen von Celebrities, Schauspielern, Künstlern und Größen der Musikszene wie Sade, Andy Warhol, Mick Jagger, Alfred Hitchcock, Clint Eastwood oder Jack Nicholson gelten heute zurecht als Ikonen der Fotografie.

Mit dem vorliegenden Buch, das im Zuge einer Ausstellung in der Kunsthalle Rostock entstand, haben wir eine Auswahl von bekannten und bisher selten veröffentlichten Bildern vorgenommen. Die Abfolge der Fotos im Buch unterstreicht die in sich ruhende Präsenz jeder einzelnen Arbeit und vermittelt ein Gefühl von Konzentration und Harmonie. Watsons Passion ist weit entfernt von der Suche nach vordergründiger Originalität. Sein Vorgehen ist geradlinig – ausschließlich definiert durch die Intelligenz des Auges und die Intuition des Augenblicks.

Eine außerordentliche Fähigkeit hat sich Albert Watson im Umgang mit dem Licht erworben. Seine Art, die Motive, insbesondere die fetischhaften Gegenstände und die Portraits, zu beleuchten, fokussiert Details und schafft eine nahezu meditative Bildatmosphäre. Wie unter einem Brennglas wird die Oberfläche nach tieferliegenden Spuren abgetastet. „Meine 'Objekte' reagieren unterschiedlich auf das Licht. Mich interessiert an diesem Vorgang die spezifische Antwort des Objekts", sagt Watson.

In letzter Zeit hat sich der Fotograf, trotz enormer Beanspruchungen mit Auftragsarbeiten umfangreichen persönlichen Projekten zugewandt. In seinem Studio, das Watson auch als Gelarie nutzt, hängen ungewöhnlich großformatige Arbeiten, aufgenommen in Las Vegas. Auf den ersten Blick überraschen die Landschaften, Interieurs und Portraits mit ihrer weichen, gefilterten Farbigkeit. Aber Watson bleibt auch in seinen neuesten Schöpfungen ganz bei sich. Auf faszinierende Weise erzeugen diese Fotografien eine Aura, die den Betrachter in das Motiv hineinversetzt, aber gleichzeitig ehrfurchtsvolle Distanz einfordert. Zweifellos, Albert Watson ist ein Künstler, der unsere Wahrnehmungen durch seine einzigartige fotografische Sicht bereichert.

Dr. Ulrich Ptak

It is nearly impossible to escape the allure of Albert Watson's photographs. Their brilliant, vivid, indeed even sublime quality puts them in a class of their own, far removed from today's excessive world of images, making them modern classics.

Watson, who discovered photography by way of studying graphic art and film, has always reflected various photographic ideas in his work, without ever adopting them. The photographer's pictorial idiom is governed by its own, unmistakable rules and ideas concerning quality. Albert Watson is a workaholic. Millions of pictures and negatives bearing the names of world-renowned magazines and companies have been amassed in his archive on New York's Washington Street. Watson's pictures of celebrities, actors, artists and musicians, such as Sade, Andy Warhol, Mick Jagger, Alfred Hitchcock, Clint Eastwood and Jack Nicholson, have rightly become icons of photography.

The images in the present volume, published on the occasion of an exhibition held at the Kunsthalle in Rostock, Germany, represent a selection of famous as well as hitherto unpublished photographs. The order in which they appear in the book serves to underscore the introspective nature of each individual work and to convey a feeling of concentration and harmony. Watson's passion could not be further removed from the search for an ostensible originality. His approach is straightforward – determined exclusively by his intelligent eye and the intuition of the moment.

Albert Watson has developed an extraordinary way of dealing with light. His method of lighting motifs, particularly fetishistic objects and subjects, entails focusing on details, which creates a well-nigh meditative mood. As if put under a magnifying glass, the surface is scanned for subliminal traces.

Despite the tremendous strain involved in carrying out commissioned assignments, the photographer has recently devoted himself to large projects of his own. Hanging in his studio, which also doubles as a gallery, are unusually large photographs that he took in Las Vegas. At first glance the soft, filtered colors of his landscapes, interiors and portraits may be surprising. Yet Watson remains true to himself, even in his latest creations. These photographs radiate an aura that draws the viewer into the picture, while at the same time demanding that distance is maintained. Albert Watson is without a doubt an artist who enriches our perception with his singular photographic vision.

Dr. Ulrich Ptak

01   Torso with 16th Century Aztec Fan

New York City
December 1990

Hinson Street

Las Vegas, Nevada
November 2001

03   Vivienne Westwood Shoe

          New York City
          1993

04   Indian, Calgary Stampede

        Canada
        July 1977

05   Philip with Duck

          Los Angeles
          1970

06   Red Car, Per Lui

            London
            1988

07   Nadege

            Paris
            1990

08   Anouk

        New York City
        1998

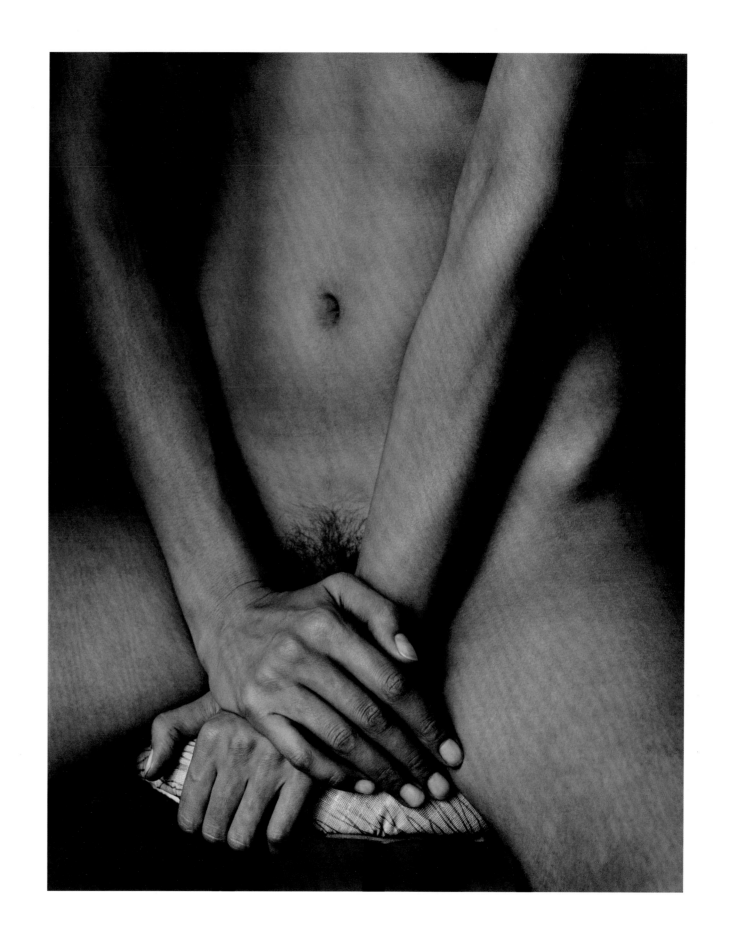

09   Breaunna Smoking

Las Vegas, Nevada
September 2000

10   Electrical Pylons, New Road off Losee

Las Vegas, Nevada
November 2001

11   Steel Worker

Beijing Locomotive Factory
June 1979

12   Michaela, Talisa, and Friend

Naples
April 1990

15   Breaunna at Bedside

          Las Vegas, Nevada
          April 2001

14   Nude

            New York City
            1988

15   Breaunna at Bedside

      Las Vegas, Nevada
      April 2001

16   Cactus

White Sands, New Mexico
November 1988

17   Police Officer

Calgary, Canada
July 1977

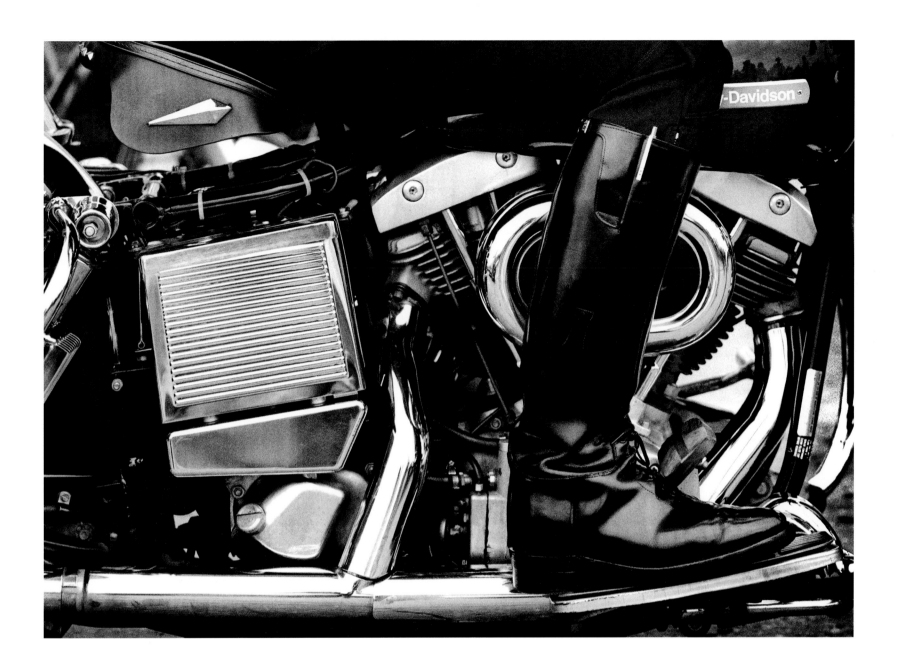

18   Dog Collar on Mannequin

        Paris
        January 1989

19   Pandora, Palomino Club

        Las Vegas, Nevada
        May 2000

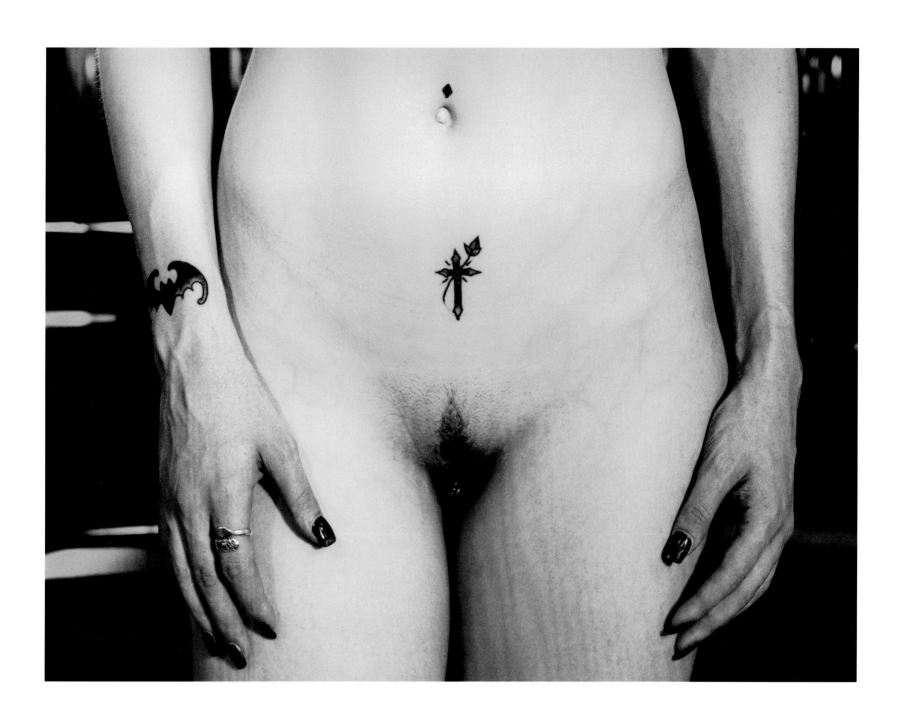

20   Monkey with Mask II

New York City
1992

21   VIP, Cheetah Room

Las Vegas, Nevada
November 1999

April 1988

23   Heel on Stovetop

Las Vegas, Nevada
September 2000

24   Carmen with Cup & Saucer

            New York City
            August 1996

25   Gabrielle Reece

            Paris
            January 1989

26   Golden Thumb Stall, circa 1323
              Found on the mummy of Tutankhamun

              Cairo Museum
              January 1990

27   Kara Young

          New York City
          February 1989

28   Chairman Mao contact sheet

Beijing
June 1979

29   15 North, off Exit 25

Las Vegas, Nevada
November 2001

30   Frank Zappa

Los Angeles
1975

31   Crosswalk outside the Beijing Hilton

      June 1979

32   Indian Competitor, Calgary Stampede

Canada
July 1977

Traci Lords with Moss Man

New Orleans
1992

34   Clark Inn Motel

Las Vegas, Nevada
September 2000

35   Mena House Swimming Pool

Giza, Egypt
February 1988

36   Andy Warhol, Christmas Card

New York City
October 1985

37   Red Hat

New York City
December 1994

40   Death Row

          Louisiana State Penitentiary
          1991

41   Chevrolet in Field

Pennsylvania
August 1988

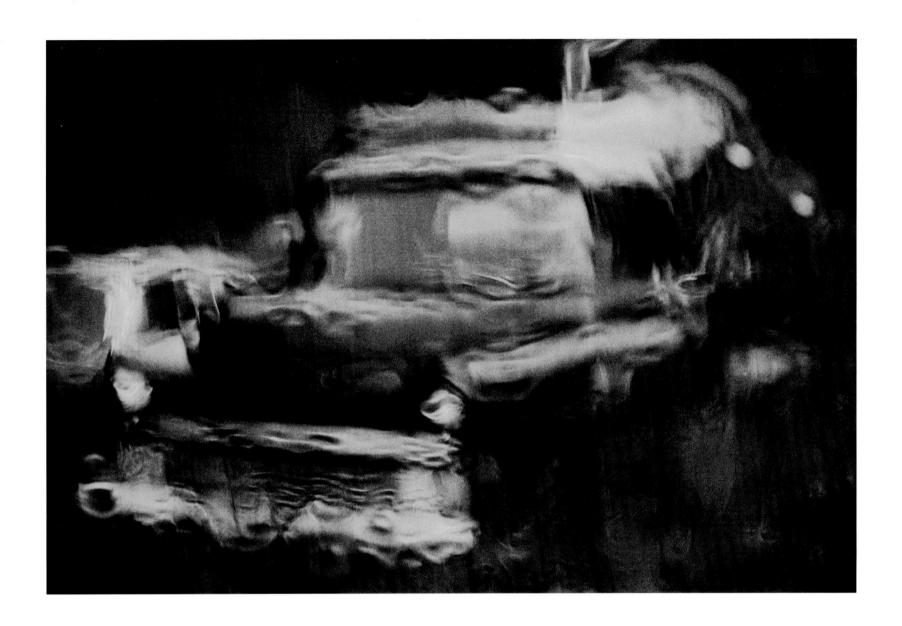

42   Charlotte in Sombrero

Arizona
February 1988

Breaunna in Front of Refrigerator

Las Vegas, Nevada
September 2000

44   Mods

London
April 1991

45   Prada

        Milan
        November 1987

46   Breaunna with Fan

New York City
December 2001

47   Charlotte
            Prada

            France
            June 1988

48   Motel on the Pennsylvania Turnpike

Pittsburgh
August 1988

49   Industria

            Milano
            October 1988

50   Breaunna in Corset

New York City
December 2001

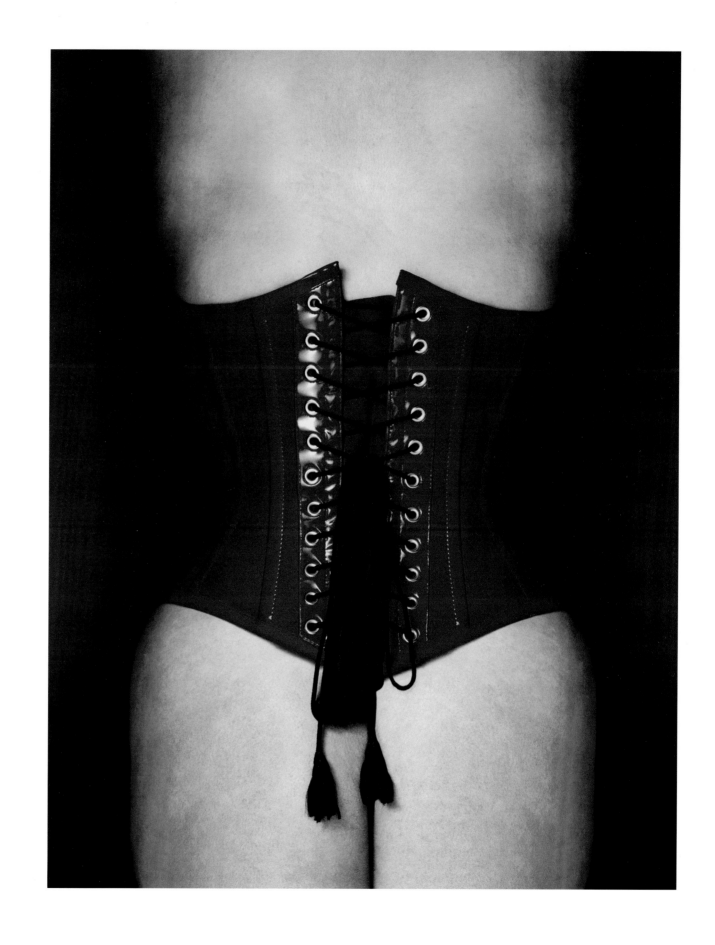

51   Anna Gitaneh

Paris Collections
December 1988

We wish to extend our special and sincere thanks to Albert Watson and his wife, Elizabeth, whose commitment to this project has been unflagging. Thanks are also due to Tasja Keetman, Albert Watson's first assistant, whose kind support was indispensable.

Dr. Ulrich Ptak

Many thanks to Ulrich Ptak without whose help none of this would have happened. Many thanks to Lothar Schirmer for his continued support. Thanks to Alexander Gelman and his staff at Design Machine. Thanks to Shin Ono at Pier 59 for so many great prints. Many thanks to the staff at The Face and Arena. Thank you Condé Nast, Rolling Stone, Stern, Max, Vibe and Interview for giving me the opportunity to make so many of these images. Thank you to all the hair and makeup artists, who contributed so much to the end product with their creativity and inspiration. Thank you to Blumarine and Prada. Thank you also to the Cairo Museum and the Louisiana State Penitentiary.

Albert Watson

Published on the occasion of the exhibition "Albert Watson"
Kunsthalle Rostock, Germany, 21 July – 1 September 2002

Exhibition sponsered by

Translations: Michele Schons

© 2002 by Albert Watson for the photographs
© 2002 by Schirmer/Mosel Munich for this edition

Design: Design Machine, New York
Lithography: Nova Concept, Berlin
Printing and binding: EBS, Verona, Italy

Die Deutsche Bibliothek – CIP-Einheitsaufnahme
Ein Titeldatensatz für diese Publikation
ist bei der Deutschen Bibliothek erhältlich.

ISBN 3-8296-0080-1

A Schirmer/Mosel Production
www.schirmer-mosel.com